The Celtic Harp

A hand-picked collection of the finest Old Airs and Dance Tunes from Ireland, Scotland, Brittanny, England, Wales, Cornwall and The Isle of Man.

Arrranged for Easy Harp, also suitable for Piano, keyboards or melody instruments.

Selected by John Loesberg
Arrangements by Christine Martin and Siobhán Bhreathnach

OSSIAN

Published by
Ossian Publications

Exclusive Distributors:
Hal Leonard
7777 West Bluemound Road, Milwaukee, WI 53213
Email: info@halleonard.com

Hal Leonard Europe Limited
42 Wigmore Street Maryleborne, London, WIU 2 RY
Email: info@halleonardeurope.com

Hal Leonard Australia Pty. Ltd.
4 Lentara Court Cheltenham, Victoria, 9132 Australia
Email: info@halleonard.com.au

Printed in EU.

www.halleonard.com

Special thanks to the helpful staff of the Dept. of Celtic
Studies, U.C.C.

Music engraving by Seton Music, Bantry.
Design by John Loesberg

Harpist Siobhán Bhreathnach

Dear Harpists and Harpers,

I trust you will find a wholesome addition to the repertoire within this small bundle of old airs from the 'Celtic' countries. Of course, one would be on rather shaky ground to claim Celtic credentials for each tune, as I have included items that can scarcely be older than the 18th or 19th centuries. As for the inclusion of some old English airs, I might point out that Celts inhabited all parts of Britain (Ancient Bretons gave London its name - Llyn-Din, Celtic for 'Lake Stronghold'), and no doubt left their influence in many spheres.

Still, it would be fairer, I suppose, to refer to the Irish/Celtic harp itself. This most responsive and versatile of instruments is enjoying quite a renaissance today and although a good few tutors and books with tunes have been published over the last fifty years, I feel that this selection of tunes may open up some new musical doors to many.

This collection could not have been produced without the expert arrangements and harmonizations of Christine Martin from the Isle of Skye and Siobhán Bhreathnach from Dublin.
Lastly - all tempo indications may be thrown to the wind! They are merely a rough guide. In fact, anything from tempo to repeats and dynamics is left to the player to experiment with.

Happy Harping!

John Loesberg

1. John O'Connor/O'Carolan/Irish*

2. The Rising of the Lark/Welsh*

3. An Alarc'h (The Swan)/Breton*

4. Sally Gardens/Irish*

5. Me a gar eur Goulmik (I love a turtle-dove)/Breton*

6. Morfa'r Frenhines (The Queen's March)/Welsh*

7. Oiche Nollag (Christmas Eve)/Irish*

8. Dydd Trwy'r Dellt (Dawn through the Wattles)/Welsh*

9. Ar Serjant-Major (The Sergeant-Major)/Breton*

10. Buain na Rainich (The Cutting of the Fern)/Scottish*

11. Come under my Plaidie/Scottish*

12. Kemp's Jig/English*

13. Hela'r 'Sgyfarnog (Hunting the Hare)/Welsh*

14. Carval ny Drogh Vraane (Jezebel Carol)/Manx**

15. Miss Loudon/Reel/Scottish**

16. Rhiwabon/Hymn/Welsh*

17. There was a Lad/Scottish*

18. The Siege of St. Malo/Cornish**

19. Miss Sally Hunter/Nathaniel Gow/Scottish*

20. The Banks of the Suir/Irish*

21. Santez Mari, Mamm Doue/Hymn/Breton**

22. The Miller's Dance/English**

23. Difyrrwch Arglwydds Owain (Lady Owen's Delight)/Welsh*

24. Doue Lan a Vadeleh/Hymn/Breton**

25. Windsor Terrace/English*

26. Putney Ferry/English**

27. Mairi Bhan Og (Mary, Young and Shy)/Scottish*

28. Ma Fransez (My Francoise)/Breton*

29. Lord Willoughby/English*

30. Sir Festus Burke/O'Carolan/Irish**

31. Follow me down to Carlow/Irish*

* Arranged by J. Loesberg & C. Martin

** Arranged by J. Loesberg & S. Bhreathnach

1 John O'Connor

Turlough O'Carolan (1670-1738)

Irish

♩. = c.63

2 The Rising of the Lark

Allegro

Welsh

leave C♮ till
end of tune

D.C.

3 An Alarc'h

(The Swan)

Andante

Breton

Set Middle C#

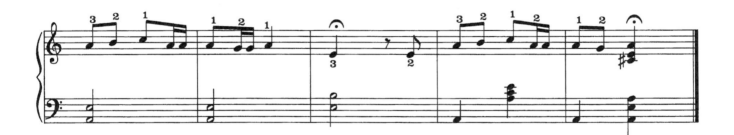

7

4 Sally Gardens

Andante $\quad \downarrow$ = c. 76

Irish

5 Me a gar eur Goulmik

Andante Moderato

(I love a Turtle-Dove)

Breton

6 Morfa'r Frenhines

Andante

(The Queen's March)

Welsh

7 Oiche Nollag

Moderato

(Christmas Eve) Single Jig

Irish

8 Dydd Trwy'r Dellt

Andante Moderato

(Dawn through the Wattles)

Welsh

9 Ar Serjant-Major

(The Sergeant-Major)

Andante

Breton

13

10 Buain na Rainich

Andante

(The cutting of the Fern)

Scottish

11 Come under my Plaidie

Scottish

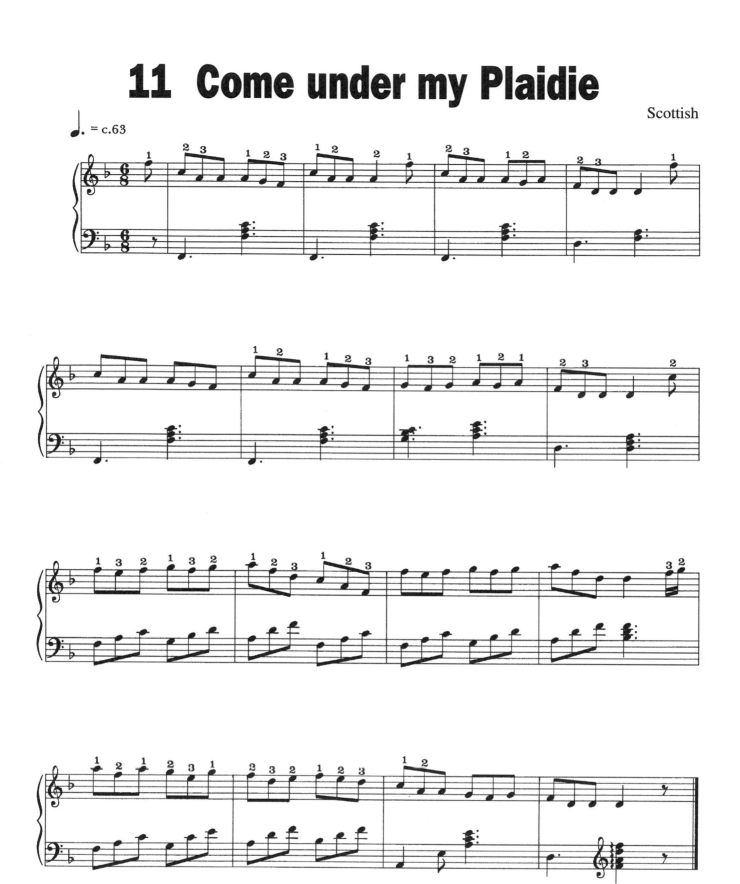

15

12 Kemp's Jig

Moderato

English

13 Hela'r 'Sgyfarnog

(Hunting the Hare)

Welsh

14 Carval ny Drogh Vraane

(Jezebel Carol)

Andante

Manx

sharpen C here

15 Miss Loudon

Allegro Moderato   Reel   Scottish

   19

16 Rhiwabon

Andante

Hymn

Welsh

17 There was a Lad

Andante

Scottish

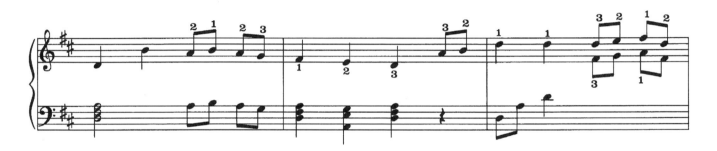

21

18 The Siege of St. Malo

Moderato

Cornish

19 Miss Sally Hunter

Nathaniel Gow (1763-1831)

Scottish

20 The Banks of the Suir

Andante

Irish

21 Santez Mari, Mamm Doue

Hymn

Breton

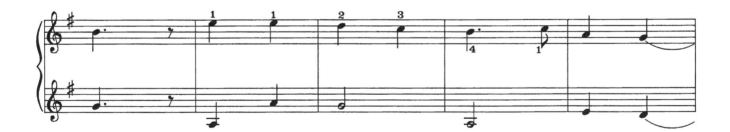

22 The Miller's Dance

Moderato

English

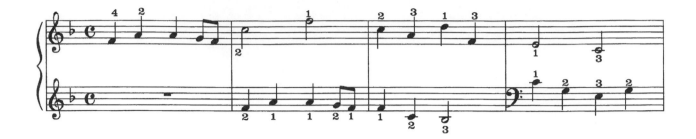

27

23 Difyrrwch Arglwydds Owain

Allegretto

(Lady Owen's Delight)

Welsh

24 Doue Lan a Vadeleh

Hymn

Breton

25 Windsor Terrace

Andante

English

26 Putney Ferry

English

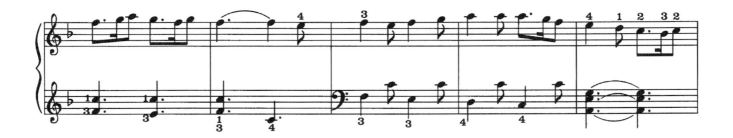

31

27 Mairi Bhan Og

(Mary, young and fair)

Scottish

Set G# above Middle C

33

28 Ma Fransez

Andante

My Françoise

Breton

29 Lord Willoughby

Moderato

English

35

30 Sir Festus Burke

Moderato

Turlough O'Carolan (1670-1738)

Irish

31 Follow me down to Carlow

Irish